Exploring Earth's Resources

Learning from Fossils

Sharon Katz Cooper

Heinemann Library
Chicago, Illinois

© 2007 Heinemann
Published by Heinemann,
a division of Reed Elsevier Inc.
Chicago, Illinois

Customer Service   888–363–4266

Visit our website at www.heinemannraintree.com

Designed by Michelle Lisseter
Printed and bound in China, by South China Printing Company

11 10 09 08 07
10 9 8 7 6 5 4 3 2 1

Library of Congress Cataloging-in-Publication Data

Katz Cooper, Sharon.
  Learning from fossils / Sharon Katz Cooper.
      p. cm. -- (Exploring Earth's resources)
  Includes index.
  ISBN-13: 978-1-4034-9317-0 (lib. bdg.)
  ISBN-10: 1-4034-9317-0 (lib. bdg.)
  ISBN-13: 978-1-4034-9325-5 (pbk.)
  ISBN-10: 1-4034-9325-1 (pbk.)
  1. Fossils--Juvenile literature. 2. Paleontology--Juvenile literature. I. Title.
  QE714.5.K38 2007
  560--dc22
                                                    2006029660

Acknowledgments
The publishers would like to thank the following for permission to reproduce photographs:
Alamy pp. **4** (Gary Crabbe), **21** (Heather Angel), **5** (Jill Stephenson); Corbis pp. **6** (Jonathan
Blair), **8** (Louie Psihoyos), **14** (Richard T. Nowitz), **17** (Layne Kennedy), **22** (Louie Psihoyos);
GeoScience Features Picture Library pp. **13** (Wade Hughes), **15** (David Bayliss); Getty Images
pp. **22** (altrendo nature); Science Photo Library pp. **9** (Manfred Kage), **10** (Vaughan Fleming),
11 (Michael Marten), **18** (Sinclair Stammers), **19** (Jim Amos), **20** (D. Van Ravenswaay), **16**
(Ted Kinsman), **22** (British Antarctic Survey), **22** (Sinclair Stammers).

Cover photograph reproduced with permission of Corbis (James L.Amos).

Contents

Some words are shown in bold, **like this**.
You can find them in the glossary on page 23.

What Are Fossils?

Fossils are all that is left of plants and animals that lived a long time ago.

Dinosaur bones are fossils.

These footprints are also fossils.

Dinosaurs left them behind.

How Are Fossils Formed?

Fossils are formed when animals die and are buried in mud.

Some fossils are formed when an animal leaves a footprint in mud.

① **dead fish**

② **fish bones** **mud**

③ **fossil**

Over a very long time, the mud becomes rock.

The animal's bones, or footprints, turn into rocks. These rocks are fossils.

Are There Different Types of Fossil?

There are fossils of many different plants and animals.

Some are huge, like this leg bone of a dinosaur.

Actual size

Other fossils are tiny. We need a **microscope** to see them.

This animal was about the size of the period at the end of this sentence.

Where Do We Find Fossils?

We often find fossils inside layers of rock.

We find them all around the world.

cliff

There are many fossils in cliffs.

These cliffs were underwater a long time ago.

We also find fossils at the bottom of the ocean.

This ship drills down into the mud and rock at the bottom of the ocean.

It brings up pieces of very old mud.

This mud holds many tiny fossils.
The fossils are the remains of
sea creatures.

13

Who Studies Fossils?

These scientists find and study fossils.

They are called **geologists** and **paleontologists**.

These scientists study rocks and
look for good places to find fossils.

How Do Scientists Collect Fossils?

Paleontologists use large tools to remove heavy rocks.

They use small tools to dig around a fossil.

They are careful not to break the fossil.

The fossil is wrapped up. It is taken to a **laboratory** to be studied.

What Can We Learn from Fossils?

Fossils can tell us about animals that no longer live on Earth.

These dinosaur egg fossils can tell us how dinosaurs had babies.

Fossils can tell us what **extinct** plants and animals looked like.

Look at the patterns in the rock. This dinosaur must have had feathers.

Fossils help us find out what happened in the past.

Scientists think a large **asteroid** hit Earth 65 million years ago.

The asteroid caused dinosaurs and other animals to become **extinct**.

Scientists learned this by studying tiny fossils.

Fossil Quiz

There are many different kinds of fossil. Which of these photos shows a fossil? (Answer on page 24.)

A

B

C

D

Glossary

 asteroid rock from space

 extinct not living on Earth anymore

 geologist scientist who studies rock

 laboratory room where a scientist works

 microscope object you use to make tiny objects look much bigger

 paleontologist scientist who finds and studies fossils

Index

Answers to quiz on page 22
All four pictures show fossils.
Photo A shows a fossil of a footprint.
Photo B shows a fossil of dinosaur eggs.
Photo C shows a fossil of a plant.
Photo D shows a fossil of fish.